Pandas Are Coming!

John Manos

Contents

Rigby®

Chapter 1

A Nice Problem to Have

What would you do if you knew that two large, strong animals were coming to live with you? What if each of these new guests weighed between 135 and 205 pounds and could possibly reach 300 pounds? What if each guest usually ate about 40 pounds of food each day? These animals have thick black and white fur and a very cute appearance. They also have long claws, sharp teeth, and very powerful jaws. Where would you put them?

This giant panda can grow to weigh as much as 300 pounds.

This is the Smithsonian National Zoo in Washington, D.C.

That's the problem the people at the Smithsonian National Zoo in Washington, D.C., faced when they learned that the pair of giant pandas they were hoping for would be arriving soon from China!

Did You Know?

Even though a panda is a rare animal, it is one of the most recognizable animals in the world.

The pandas coming to the National Zoo were named Tian Tian® and Mei Xiang®. Tian Tian is a male, and Mei Xiang is a female. (They had been introduced while living at the China Research and Conservation Center for the Giant Panda in Wolong where they were born.)

Pandas at the China Research and Conservation Center for the Giant Panda in Wolong live in enclosed areas.

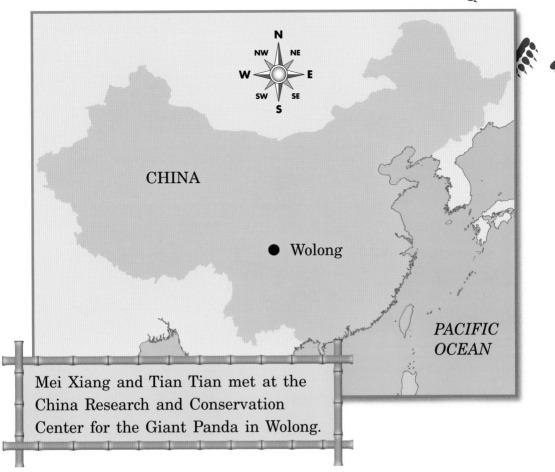

CHINA

Wolong

PACIFIC
OCEAN

Mei Xiang and Tian Tian met at the
China Research and Conservation
Center for the Giant Panda in Wolong.

The people at the zoo were excited that the
pandas were coming. They wanted them to be
content and healthy in their new home. They
decided to remodel the zoo's old panda house and
yards to create a more interesting environment for
the young pandas. It would be an enormous job
and would cost nearly 2 million dollars. But Tian
Tian and Mei Xiang were worth it!

Chapter 2

What's the Plan?

It would be almost a five-month wait before the pandas would leave China. That sounded like enough time, but there was so much to do that the zoo planners had to hurry.

Quickly they had to decide what to do. First they would meet and consider all of the things that the panda house and outdoor yards would need. Next they would make a plan for remodeling the building. Then they would make sure that the plan met all of the needs they had identified. Finally they would hire the builders and start building!

They knew from the start that the panda exhibit had to do four things:

- provide a healthy and safe home for the pandas
- provide an interesting environment
- allow zoo workers to care for and study the pandas
- let people see the pandas and learn more about them.

How to Make a Great Giant Panda Exhibit

- Understand the problem.
- Plan to solve the problem.
- Solve the problem.
- Look back.
- Check the results.

People at the zoo may have used these problem-solving steps to help them build the right home for the new pandas.

7

Thinking About Pandas

The planners decided that if they understood more about how pandas lived in the wild, they would have a better idea about what pandas might need in the zoo.

In the wild, pandas live in the wet mountains of central China. They don't live in groups or even in pairs and may go months without seeing another panda. The only pandas that spend a lot of time together are mothers and their cubs.

A mother panda spends a lot of time taking care of her baby.

Giant pandas hold on tightly to bamboo as they eat it.

Bamboo makes up 95 percent of a panda's diet, and when they are awake, pandas spend most of their time eating. Wild pandas might have to travel far in search of fresh bamboo, and they get plenty of exercise as they travel many miles looking for it. The rest of the time they sleep.

Chapter 3

What Do We Need?

Tian Tian and Mei Xiang had been born in a panda research center and had met each other before. Female pandas often climb trees to avoid male pandas, so the zoo put many trees in their yards. Zoo workers hoped that Tian Tian and Mei Xiang would not mind being around each other, especially while they were cubs. These people also hoped that the pandas would become parents someday.

Female pandas stay away from male pandas by climbing trees.

The planners made a list of what the new panda house would need, based on their knowledge and understanding of pandas. It would have to include enough space for each panda to live separately but also space that they could share if they wanted. It would also need places for the pandas to rest and sleep, to exercise, and to keep cool. It would also need to have a place to store a one-week supply of bamboo and keep it fresh.

Pandas and People

Next the planners thought about people. Most people love pandas, so they thought that visitors should be able to see Tian Tian and Mei Xiang in their new home. People would probably want to learn more about pandas, too. Researchers would need to study Tian Tian and Mei Xiang, and zookeepers would need to care for them.

People who study animals need to watch them for a long time and make notes about what they see.

The planners decided that to meet the needs of all these people, the new panda house would have to include areas for zookeepers to prepare food for the pandas and areas for researchers to work. There would also need to be ways for researchers to study the pandas. Finally it would be necessary to have places for visitors to watch and learn about the pandas.

Did You Know?

- There are three zoos in the United States that have giant pandas.
- Tian Tian and Mei Xiang have different markings. Tian Tian looks as if he is wearing short black socks up to his knees, while Mei Xiang looks as if she has long black stockings. Tian Tian has two black dots across his nose. Mei Xiang has a pale black line of fur across the top of her nose.

Chapter 4

Building a Panda Place

Finally it was time for the planners to begin working on the plans for the pandas' new home. Many people, such as those who knew about water, cooling, and electric systems were involved in this work.

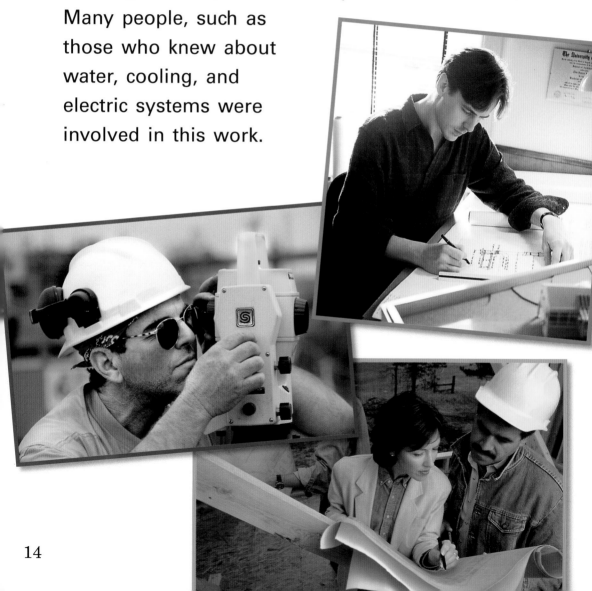

Panda specialists helped figure out how to make the panda house a nice place for Tian Tian and Mei Xiang to live. They wanted people to be able to see the pandas, but they wanted some privacy for the pandas, too. They especially wanted to be sure that the pandas would be able to survive the hot summer weather of Washington, D.C. Plants and trees would provide privacy and shade.

Figure It Out

One panda in a zoo needs about 8,000 square feet of outdoor space. Since two pandas were coming to the National Zoo, about how big would the total outdoor area need to be? Can you figure it out?

Answer: 8,000 x 2 = 16,000 square feet

After months of work, the design for the new panda house was ready. It seemed like the new panda home would have everything, including indoor and outdoor spaces for each panda. There would be a fence with a gate in the middle of the outdoor space. The keepers could open the gate to give the pandas time to be together.

Outside there would be shade trees and machines that would spray cool mist over the pandas. There would be cold caves, water pools, and sand pits for the pandas to play in.

Indoors the pandas' space would be cooled. Visitors could look through large windows to see the pandas up close. The pandas could go into their dens when they wanted to be alone. There was also a kitchen where zookeepers could make food for the pandas. There were also spaces for a research center, a video system, and displays to teach people about the pandas.

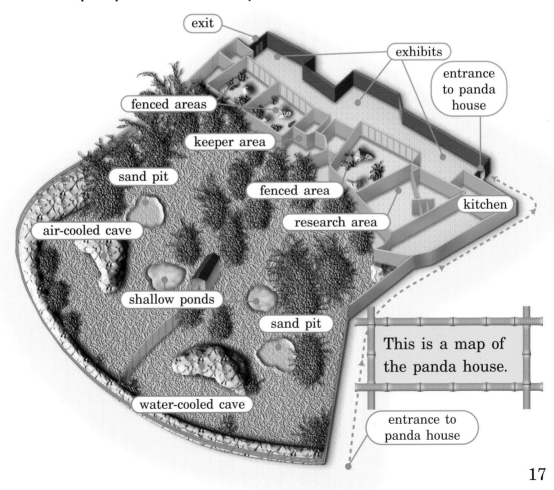

exit

exhibits

entrance to panda house

fenced areas

keeper area

sand pit

fenced area

kitchen

air-cooled cave

research area

shallow ponds

sand pit

This is a map of the panda house.

water-cooled cave

entrance to panda house

The designers built a rough model of the rocks that would be included in the panda place. The model was a way for the designers to check their work. It also helped them design the pandas' rock caves by giving them a better idea of what the caves would look like when they were built instead of just seeing a picture of them on paper.

The people at the zoo created this model of the outdoor spaces in the panda exhibit.

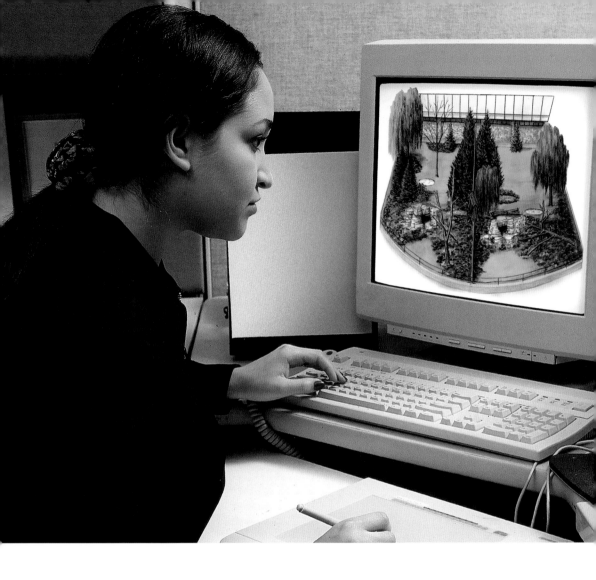

Designers sometimes create models using computers. A model on a computer can allow the designers to feel as if they are walking through a building before it is built.

19

Chapter 5

A New Life in the Zoo

The designers checked and rechecked the design to make sure that it met all of the needs of both the pandas and the people. Looking back and checking is an important part of problem solving. It's easy to correct mistakes when the design is still on paper, but difficult when something is already built.

When at last everyone was sure the design was the best it could be, the planning part of the project was over. Building of the pandas' new home could begin!

Many people helped build the panda exhibit. One group built the caves, while another group created a system that made the fog and mist. Many volunteers came to help plant trees and bushes. There were a lot of people who cared about those two pandas!

21

The real test of whether the zoo had found a good answer to the panda house problem came when Tian Tian and Mei Xiang arrived. No giant pandas had lived in the zoo since 1999. Would they like it and feel comfortable enough to continue their normal habits, such as eating and sleeping?

The pandas sat in their dens and relaxed on the rocks in their caves. They tried out the pools and avoided the sand pits.

They found food treats hidden by their keepers and ate lots and lots of bamboo. The pandas seemed to be content in their new home. Zoo scientists collected information on what the pandas liked and disliked to learn how to build even better homes for giant pandas.

After almost 13 months of designing and building, the new giant panda house and outdoor yards opened on January 10, 2001. People loved the new panda exhibit. More than 35,000 people came to see Tian Tian and Mei Xiang on the first weekend that the panda house was open.

The zoo set up a Web camera and a Web site so that panda fans could see photos, read daily reports, and view the pandas' activities. By the end of the year, over 2 million people had visited the pandas! It's likely that the panda exhibit will continue to be a popular place for a very long time.

Index